KU-053-444

# Note to Parents and Teachers

The READING ABOUT: STARTERS series introduces key science vocabulary to young children while encouraging them to discover and understand the world around them. The series works as a set of graded readers in three levels.

LEVEL 2: BEGIN TO READ ALONE follows guidelines set out in the National Curriculum for Year 2 in schools. These books can be read alone or as part of guided or group reading. Each book has three sections:

• Information pages that introduce key words. These key words appear in bold for easy recognition on pages where the related science concepts are explained.
• A lively story that recalls this vocabulary and encourages children to use these words when they talk and write.
• A quiz and index ask children to look back and recall what they have read.

# Questions for Further Investigation

SWITCH IT ON explains key concepts about USING ELECTRICITY. Here are some suggestions for further discussion linked to the questions on the information spreads:

p. 5 *Do you know where trains get their electricity from?* Ask children to look at picture – train gets electricity from wires. Electricity flows along wires from a power station.

p. 7 *Why are electric wires put up in the air or underground?* Electricity is very dangerous so most wires are put where people cannot easily touch them.

p. 9 *What happens if this woman pulls out the plug again?* Reinforce the idea that electricity can only flow to the machine when it is connected, e.g. by a wire or lead.

p. 11 *What do electric machines do in your home?* Ask children to make a list, grouping machines by room or by what they do, e.g. light, sound, computers, moving machines.

p. 13 *Why are there few switches or sockets in a bathroom?* Explain that electricity flows easily in water, so it is easy to get a shock in a bathroom if you are wet from washing. That's why bathroom lights are often turned on with a long cord not a switch.

p. 15 *Why are batteries different sizes?* Some jobs need more energy. A watch doesn't need much energy, so a small battery will do. A torch needs more energy – and bigger batteries.

p. 19 *Can you guess what happens when electric wires are damaged in a storm?* Explain that blown over poles/cut wires can create a break in the circuit, causing a power cut.

p. 21 *Why do you think a bus or space shuttle can't use a lead?* How long would they be?

p. 23 *Where in the world would solar panels work best?* Sunny places! And wind farms?

---

## ADVISORY TEAM

**Educational Consultant**
**Andrea Bright** – Science Co-ordinator, Trafalgar Junior School, Twickenham

**Literacy Consultant**
**Jackie Holderness** – former Senior Lecturer in Primary Education, Westminster Institute, Oxford Brookes University

**Series Consultants**
**Anne Fussell** – Early Years Teacher and University Tutor, Westminster Institute, Oxford Brookes University

**David Fussell** – C.Chem., FRSC

# CONTENTS

© Aladdin Books Ltd 2005

*Designed and produced by*
Aladdin Books Ltd
2/3 Fitzroy Mews
London W1T 6DF

*First published in*
Great Britain in 2005 by
Franklin Watts
96 Leonard Street
London EC2A 4XD

A catalogue record for this
book is available from the
British Library.

ISBN 0 7496 6246 8

Printed in Malaysia

All rights reserved

**Editor:** Sally Hewitt

**Design:** Flick, Book Design
and Graphics

Thanks to:
• The pupils of Trafalgar
Infants School, Twickenham for
appearing as models in this book.
• Luke, Hugh and Sara Pullman for
appearing as models in the story.
• Lynne Thompson for helping
to organise the photoshoots.
• The pupils and teachers
of Trafalgar Junior School,
Twickenham and St. Nicholas
C.E. Infant School, Wallingford,
for testing the sample books.

Photocredits:
l-left, r-right, b-bottom, t-top,
c-centre, m-middle
Cover tl & tr, 3, 9tr, 10tr, 13tr,
14ml, 16 all, 18tr, 19, 20, 24 both,
26 all, 27mr, 27bl, 28 both, 29,
30tl, 31br, 31bc — Jim Pipe. Cover
b, 2tl, 2bl, 5br, 8, 10b, 13b, 14mr,
14br, 15 all, 17 both, 18b, 22m, 31bl
— Marc Arundale/Select Pictures.
2ml, 5m, 30tr — Corel. 4tr, 14tr,
25mr, 25bl, 27tl, 31ml — Corbis.
4b, 11m, 23 both — Photodisc. 6tr
— Comstock. Cover tm, 6b, 22tr,
22bl — European Community. 7tr
— Brand X Pictures. 7b — PBD. 9b
— Flick Smith. 11br, 14bl, 32 —
Ingram Publishing. 21tl — Ballard
Bus Program. 21b — NASA. 25tr
— Hugh Pullman.

# USING ELECTRICITY

# Switch It On

## By Jim Pipe

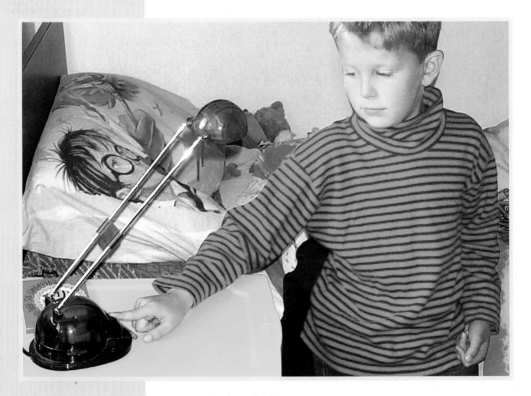

Aladdin/Watts
London • Sydney

Everything needs **energy** to work and move.

Cars and trucks get **energy** from fuel.

Electric **machines** get **energy** from **electricity**.

**Fuel**

You get your energy from food and drink.

4

Electric **machines** can be small, like an alarm clock, or big, like a train.

Powerful trains need a lot of **energy**. They use a lot of **electricity**.

**Train**

A CD player only needs a little **electricity**.

• Do you know where trains get their electricity from?

Electricity comes from a power station.
It **flows** along **wires** into our homes.

Tall poles and **pylons** carry
the **wires** up in the air.
Can you see any **wires**
outside your house?

**Pylons**

Never fly a kite
where there
are electric
wires in the air.

6

**Wires** carry electricity around your home.

Most of these **wires** are under the ground or in the walls of your house.

We use electricity at home, at school and at work.

Electricity **flows** all day and night. You can turn on a light or TV at any time.

• Why are electric wires put up in the air or underground?

Wires in the walls carry electricity from **switches** to lights.

You press a **switch** one way to turn a light on. You press it the other way to turn a light off.

**Switch**

Wires also carry electricity to **sockets**.
We **plug** machines into **sockets** to
make them work.

Electricity flows from
the **socket** along the
**lead**. This is a wire
that goes to the
machine.

**Plugging in**

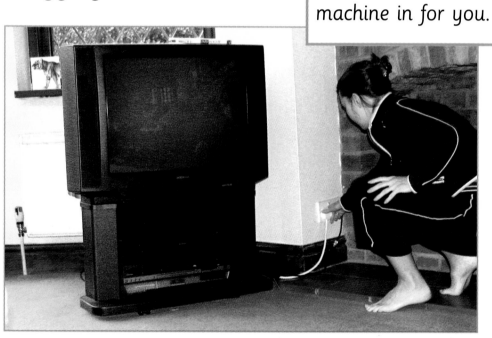

Always ask an adult
to plug an electric
machine in for you.

• What happens if this woman pulls out the plug again?

Electricity is very useful.
Machines use electricity to
do many different things.

Lamps give off **light**.
Radios and televisions
make **sound** and pictures.

Ovens and hair dryers **heat** things up.
Fridges and freezers make them cold.

**Hair dryer**

Look around your house. What machines must you plug in?

**Computer**

Some machines like torches use electricity but don't need to be plugged in.

Simple machines like staplers and scissors don't need electricity at all.

**Stapler**

• What do electric machines do in your home?

Electricity from a socket is called **mains** electricity. It is very dangerous. If **mains** electricity flowed into you it would give you a nasty **shock**. It could even kill you.

**Danger! Electricity**

**BE SAFE:** this sign tells you to watch out for electricity.

Always use electric machines **safely**:

Machines like toasters can get very hot. So don't touch!

• Never play with machines that plug in.
• Never touch anything electric with wet hands.
• Ask an adult to plug machines in for you.
• Keep electric objects away from babies.

• Why are there few switches or sockets in a bathroom?

Some electric machines use **batteries**. A **battery** stores electricity. When this is used up, we say the **battery** has run out.

Bigger **batteries** store more energy. Can you guess the right **battery** for these machines?

Cars use big batteries to start their engine and to shine their lights.

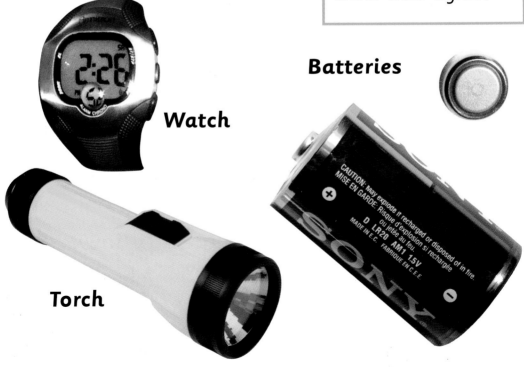

**Watch**

**Torch**

**Batteries**

14

If you look at a **battery**, see if you can find the signs **+** and **—** .

**+** shows the **positive** end of a battery.
**—** shows the **negative** end of a battery.

The **battery** must be the right way around for a machine to work.

• Why are batteries different sizes?

The wires in walls join together to make a **circuit**.

A **circuit** means a loop. It has no loose ends. Electricity flows around and around the loop.

A simple **circuit** is made up of a battery pack, a **bulb**, a **bulb holder** and two wires.

**Battery pack**

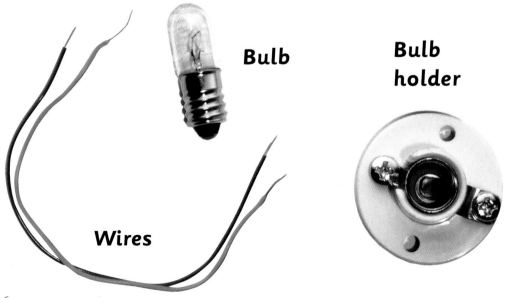

**Bulb**

**Bulb holder**

**Wires**

Join one end of each wire to the battery pack.

Join the other ends to the **bulb holder** and screw in the **bulb**.

Will the bulb light up?

Connect a buzzer to a circuit. The electricity makes it buzz.

• Can you see the loop made by this circuit?
Follow it around with your finger.

What if the bulb does not light? Perhaps the wires don't touch the battery, or **connect**. This is a **break** in the circuit.

**Break**

If the wires are attached to the same ends of the bulb holder, the bulb is not part of the loop, or circuit. It won't light!

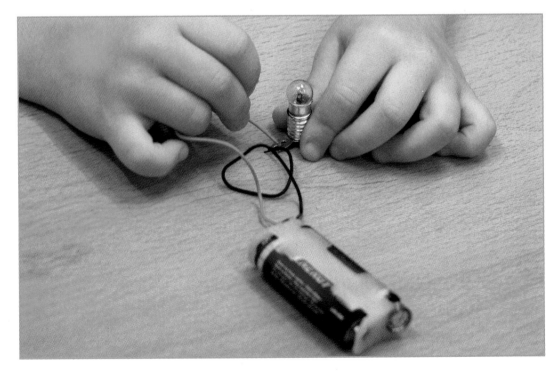

Do you know how a switch works?

When you press a switch, you make a **break** in the circuit. The bulb goes off.

When you press the switch the other way, the wires **connect** and the bulb goes on!

• Can you guess what happens when electric wires are damaged in a storm?

Electricity can also make things move.

Electric **motors** make these toy cars whizz around a track. Can you see the circuits they are connected to?

The train on page 4 has a **motor.** It gets its electricity from the wires above it.

This bus also has an electric **motor.** But it gets its energy from batteries.

The scientific name for a battery is a **cell.** **Cells** give a shuttle energy out in space.

**Space shuttle**

Why do you think a bus or space shuttle can't use a lead?

We make electricity in different ways. A **power station** burns fuels like coal and oil.

**Coal**

This machine looks like a big fan. When the wind blows, the machine spins.

This turns a **turbine,** which makes electricity when it moves.

22

Storm clouds can make electricity called **lightning**. You see a flash of light.

The **lightning** jumps from the clouds to the ground.

Then you hear a rumbling sound. This is thunder!

Solar panels make electricity when the Sun shines on them.

• Where in the world would solar panels work best?

# POWER CUT!

Look out for words about **electricity**.

Mum was in the kitchen when the two boys ran in.

"It's raining," said Hugh. "Can we play with our **electric** cars?"

"Dry your hands first," said Mum.

Mum **plugged** the **lead** into the **socket**. Hugh pressed the **switch**. His car shot off the track!

"It won't work now," said Luke. "The **motor** needs **electricity** from the track to make it go."

Then Uncle Jim came in. "May I borrow that **lead**?" he asked. "The **batteries** have run out in my radio."

"Only if you're quick!" joked Hugh.

"I just want to hear the news," said Uncle Jim.

"There's a storm coming."

"Cool! That means **lightning**," said Hugh.

"Yes," said Uncle Jim. "We should stay **safe** indoors. **Lightning** can be dangerous."

25

"What if the **lightning** cuts
off the power?" asked Luke.
"It will be dark soon."

"Here's my torch," said Hugh.
He **switched** it on.
But nothing happened!

"Turn the **batteries**
the other way round,"
said Mum.
"Look at the **positive**
and **negative** signs."

Still nothing happened!

"Try this new **bulb**,"
said Uncle Jim.

Luke screwed it in.
The torch worked!

Thunder rumbled nearby. "Uh-oh," said Hugh.

Suddenly, there was big flash and a loud bang. All the **lights** went off!

Uncle Jim tried the **switch**. "No luck," he said.

"It's a power cut. The **lightning** may have hit the **wires** from the **power station**."

"The phone is dead too," said Mum.

"Use your mobile," said Luke. "It runs on **batteries** and **connects** without a **lead**."

Mum **lighted** some candles. "Don't knock them over," she said.

"I'm a bit cold now," said Luke.
"Is the **heating** on?"

"No. It's **electric,** too," said Mum.
"And so is the cooker!"

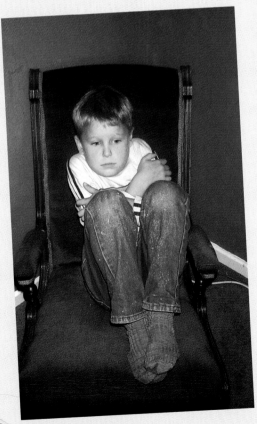

"Don't worry," said Uncle Jim. "People all over the world live without **electricity**. They use wood or oil for **heat** and **light**. So can we!"

Uncle Jim brought in some wood and **lighted** the fire.

Luke and Hugh sat next to the fire.
"Not too close," said Uncle Jim.

"We can toast some bread on it too,"
said Mum.

"I'm bored," said Hugh. "Can we watch TV?"
"It's **electric** too, silly," said Luke.

"We don't need **electricity** to play cards,"
said Uncle Jim.
"The winner gets the first piece of toast!"
shouted Hugh.

Suddenly, the **lights** came on. "Great! The **mains** electricity must be back on," said Mum.

"Too bad," said Hugh. "I liked playing in the dark!"

"Me too," said Luke. "But now I know how much we use **electricity**. Without power, we wouldn't have TVs, CDs or computer games!"

Write a list of **electric** machines that **plug** in or use **batteries**. Draw pictures of how you use these **machines** at home or at school.

I switch on a lamp.

I listen to my CD player.

# QUIZ

What gives this train **energy**?

Answer on page 5

What does this **safety** sign mean?

Answer on page 12

What do cars use a **battery** for?

Answer on page 14

What do these electric objects do?

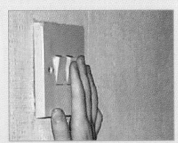

**Bulb**          **Switch**                    **Battery**

Have you read this book? Well done! Do you remember these words? Look back and find out.

# INDEX